THE MORRIS BOOK A HISTORY OF MORRIS DANCING, WITH A DESCRIPTION OF ELEVEN DANCES AS PERFORMED BY THE MORRIS-MEN OF ENGLAND • VOLUME 1 • SHARP, CECIL J.

Publisher's Note

Purchase of this book entitles you to a free trial membership in the publisher's book club at www.rarebooksclub.com. (Time limited offer.) Simply enter the barcode number from the back cover onto the membership form on our home page. The book club entitles you to select from millions of books at no additional charge. You can also download a digital copy of this and related books to read on the go. Simply enter the title or subject onto the search form to find them.

Note: This is an historic book. Pages numbers, where present in the text, refer to the first edition of the book and may also be in indexes.

If you have any questions, could you please be so kind as to consult our Frequently Asked Questions page at www.rarebooksclub.com/faqs.cfm? You are also welcome to contact us there.
Publisher: General Books LLC™, Memphis, TN, USA, 2012. ISBN: 9781153714174.
Proofreading: pgdp.net

MORRIS DANCERS, AS DEPICTED IN AN OLD STAINED GLASS WINDOW IN A HOUSE AT BETLEY, STAFFORDSHIRE.

THE MORRIS BOOK

A HISTORY OF MORRIS DANCING WITH A DESCRIPTION OF ELEVEN DANCES AS PERFORMED BY THE MORRIS-MEN OF ENGLAND

BY
CECIL J. SHARP
AND HERBERT C. MACILWAINE
IN TWO PARTS. PART I.
LONDON NOVELLO AND COMPANY, LTD. 1907.

This Book is issued in connection with "Morris Dance Tunes," by the same Authors

(Sets I. and II., price 2/- each.)
LONDON: NOVELLO AND COMPANY, LTD.

TO OUR FRIENDS AND PUPILS
The Members of the Espérance Girls' Club,
CUMBERLAND MARKET, N.W.

PREFACE.

Besides other friends, too numerous for individual mention, who have given us able and willing help in the writing of this book, we desire to tender especial thanks to the following: To the Lady Isabel Margesson, by means of whose kind assistance we were enabled to note certain of the dances herein described; to Miss Florence Warren, whose help was simply invaluable; and to the Rev. S. Baring Gould, for permission to reproduce in our text the old woodcut of the historic Kemp, who danced the Morris steps all the way from London to Norwich.

CONTENTS

INTRODUCTION 2

HISTORICAL 4

Bibliography 7

MORRIS DANCE TUNES 8

Notes on Morris Tunes 8

THE DANCE 9

The Morris Step 9

Diagrams of Morris Steps (explaining Notation-marks) 11

Positions, and Change of Position (Diagrams) 11

Evolutions 12

Down-and-Back; and Up-and-Back . 12

The Chain (Diagrams) 13

Cross-over (Diagrams) 13

Back-to-Back (Diagrams) 14

Go-and-come 14

The Ring 14

Steps in Foregoing Evolutions 14

The Jump (explaining Notation-marks, &c.) 14

The Hands (movements described) .. 15

The Call 16

Length of Dances (how to shorten or extend) 16

SPECIAL INSTRUCTIONS FOR VARIOUS DANCES:— 16

BEAN-SETTING 16

To Form Ring (Diagrams) 16

Dibbing 16

COUNTRY GARDENS 17

Notation of Hand-striking 17

CONSTANT BILLY 17

Diagram of Stick-tapping 17

RIGS O'MARLOW 17

Diagrams of Stick-tapping 17

BLUFF KING HAL 18

Description of step, and manner of dancing 18

HOW D'YE DO? 18

Description, and note on singing 18

SHEPHERD'S HEY 19

Instructions for Stick-tapping and Diagram of Hand-clapping 19

On holding sticks 19

NOTATION (Detailed instructions for all the Dances described):— 19

BEAN-SETTING (Stick Dance) 20

LAUDNUM BUNCHES (Corner Dance) 20

COUNTRY GARDENS (Handkerchief Dance) 20

CONSTANT BILLY (Stick Dance) 21

TRUNKLES (Corner Dance) 21

RIGS O'MARLOW (Stick Dance) .. 22

BLUFF KING HAL (Handkerchief Dance) 23

HOW D'YE DO? (Corner Dance) ... 24

SHEPHERD'S HEY (Stick or Handkerchief Dance) 25

BLUE-EYED STRANGER (Handkerchief Dance) 25

MORRIS OFF 25

INTRODUCTION.

We have been drawn to the publication of tunes and description of the old English Morris, not primarily for the information of the archæologist and scholar, but to help those who may be disposed to restore a vigorous and native custom to its lapsed pre-eminence.

Whether we have erred in believing that there exists to-day a wide and keen desire for that restoration will be plainly shown in the reception and the result of our endeavour. How we ourselves came by the belief in that desire is easily told.

The idea that the Morris dance might once again be known amongst us, in town and countryside, as the ordered expression of a national spirit, was given to us in this wise. One of us—it is not by now too much to claim—had acquired an enthusiasm for Folk-music, and a certain knack of finding it where it still survived in the agèd memories of the peasantry, and of transcribing and preserving it when found. The other had also his knack of passing on the music that pleased him to susceptible and willing juniors, and of making them to perform the same. In a happy hour the collector with his treasury and the teacher, pining for some fresher and sincerer melodies, met together. The "Folk Songs from Somerset" were given to those working girls of London town to whom this book is dedicated. From the very start we were aware that the old songs, merry or mournful, that until then had been looked upon by this newer generation for the greater part with something of an antiquarian and merely curious eye, had been given wings and a new vitality. The songs of peasant-folk long dead, songs of love and war, parting and death, prospered and spread in the London streets and workrooms like the news of victory. We were very well used to find in these singers apt and willing learners; we were also used to note that whatsoever we had found to teach them hitherto, passed, when the performance was done, into forgetfulness: we were totally unused to find this fertility and resonance follow, as it followed upon the teaching of the Folk-songs. It was like a sowing and a full harvest in a place where, until now, we had tilled all but unavailingly.

Forbye Folk-songs, the collector had noted, some seven years before, a set of Morris tunes from Kimber, leader of the Headington (Oxon) men; these had lain until now unused. Seeing the Folk-music fall upon such good ground and flourish so amazingly, even amongst these quick-witted Londoners, strangers to the countryside, it naturally suggested itself to him that here was the opportunity, so long desired, to wake the Morris from its long sleep. Anybody not deaf and blind, or unobservant as a stone, knows that the genius of dancing is born in the London girl of the people, as surely as in children of the sun.

We had Kimber and his cousin up to town; and the result of their coming far outran our fondest anticipations. The Morris, like that magic beanstalk, seemed to outwit the laws of nature: we saw it in the heart of London rise up from its long sleep before our very eyes. In connection with this affair, the mention of that well-beloved fable is appropriate and irresistible. The first dance that was set before these Londoners—upon this occasion which we enthusiasts make bold to call historic—was Bean-setting. It represents the setting of the seed in springtime. Of course the music, its lilt and the steps that their forefathers had footed to it in the olden time, were as little known to these, the London born, as the tongue and ceremonial of old Peru. As little known, yet not strange at all; it was a summons never heard until now, yet instantly obeyed; because, though unfamiliar and unforeseen, it was of England and came, even though it was centuries upon the way, to kinsfolk. Let the precisian explain it as he may, that is our way of accounting for an experience both fruitful and astounding. Within half an hour of the coming of these Morris-men we saw the Bean-setting—its thumping and clashing of staves, its intricate figures and steps hitherto unknown—full swing upon a London floor. And upon the delighted but somewhat dazed confession of the instructor, we saw it perfect in execution to the least particular. Perfect, yet in a different order of perfection from that attainable by men. It may be noted here and now by all who have to do with the instruction of girls in the Morris, that the feminine temperament inevitably robs the dance of something of its sturdiness. It is nothing to lament; for what is lost in vigour is assuredly more than made good in gracefulness. At any rate, there was Bean-setting, perfect in its kind. No wonder Jack-and-the-Beanstalk came to mind and stayed there with the memory of this evening.

It was even so with all the other dances: to see them shown was to see them learned. And the Folk-songs had prepared us for what followed: here was no mere fugitive delight and curiosity, as of a child with a new toy. We had given back to these children of the city no less than a birthright long mislaid.

The Morris-men came in October. In the following February, 1906, the songs and dances were performed before a company of friends. The audience, if very friendly, was also very critical; and there was represented in it, literally, every element in contemporary society. And every element, or representatives of each, exhorted us to give our performance in public, since it was so good that the world in general must know of it.

In April, 1906, we did so. The performance was given very nearly in the height of the concert season; in no announcement of it was any mention made of charity, or any lack or need of funds: the entertainment was run as a public affair. And the public responded so that we filled the hall to the doors and were reluctantly constrained to refuse admittance to a host beside. The entertainment has since then been repeated several times; and every repetition brought substantial evidence of continually increasing public interest.

It should be mentioned here that Miss Mary Neal, of the Espérance Working Girls' Club, not only made the venture possible in the beginning, but, with her powers of help and organization, gave it a reach and strength that neither of us could have given.

But outside appreciation did not end here—one might really say that it only began. Inquiries poured in from every quarter of the Kingdom, from every class and kind of person. They all wanted to know how they also might be shown the way to do as we had done—revive these traditional English songs and dances in their neighbourhood, amongst the rising generation of English men and women. One of the inquiries, as to how the Morris dances might be imported there, came from Japan, where all things typically English are in so great request.

FROM THE FRONTISPIECE OF "KEMP'S NINE DAIES WONDER, PERFORMED ON A JOURNEY FROM LONDON TO NORWICH."

In the case of the Folk-songs, it was easy enough to instruct the anxious inquirer. But as to the Morris dances it was otherwise. Here there were no handbooks to recommend, for the sufficient reason that not one existed. With ourselves, and with the few—Alas! very few—traditional Morris-men left in England, there reposed the only practical knowledge of the dances in existence. With all the goodwill in the world we could only give them to others as the Morris-men gave them to us—by example, since in the shape of printed precept there was nothing. So far as possible this demand for tuition of the dances has been, and is being, met. Some of the girls already mentioned are teaching or have taught the dances in many London centres and here and there in eight counties at least, including Monmouth and Derby, Devon and Norfolk, and the Home Counties. But the demand is great and growing, the supply is obviously limited. In London alone it might be met, or nearly so; but in the provinces, with existing or possible resources, it cannot be, even if we could command the services of the spirited, historic Kemp, who danced the Morris all the way from London to Norwich—*see* plate opposite. This indefatigable traveller, incidentally, is somewhat curiously figurative of this latter-day revival of the Morris—of its restoration by townsfolk to dwellers in the country.

Thus we were faced with a sudden demand and very limited means wherewith to meet it. In these circumstances we naturally bethought ourselves of possible expedients. To us it seemed practicable to meet it only in one way—through the writing of a book on Morris dancing, by the help of which even those who had never seen the dances performed might be enabled to learn them, and so pass them on. The result of our endeavours must declare itself in the efforts of others to make use of this little handbook. That there is a demand for it is very sure: whether we have succeeded in putting together an intelligible and a workable manual of dances—notoriously a very hard thing to do—will be told presently in the tally of practising Morris-dancers in England—and Japan. We have aimed at simplicity, brevity and clearness in the description.

As to the extent of the demand and its constant tendency to increase, so far, there can be no doubt. As to the permanence of the demand, as to whether the Morris dance is likely to become again, as once it was, a feature of our national life, one can only surmise. For ourselves, we believe absolutely in the permanence of this revival, and that these astounding results of our efforts hitherto are evidence, not of a fleeting phase or vogue but of no less than that we have restored to our own people a rightful inheritance, a means and method of self-expression in movement, native and sincere, such as is offered by no other form of dancing known to us.

The outstanding feature of all our English institutions is their continuity: to have continuity you must have age and a hallowed tradition: these we have in everything national, save only in our songs and dances. These, although we are anything but an imitative race, we have imported from un-English lands, with the inevitable result that in dance and music we express everybody but ourselves. We shall go on doing so until the treasure-house of our Folk-music and dances—now for several generations mysteriously closed to us—shall be re-opened. In this handbook we have tried to do something towards restoring that forsaken repository to its rightful pre-eminence.

HISTORICAL.

We claim for this sketch no completeness: we are chiefly concerned with the Morris as a lapsed yet living art, calling, as we hold, for revival; we look to the Morris-men, not primarily as subject-matter for the industrious archæologist, but as heralds to the sweetening of the town life of England and the re-peopling of her forsaken countryside. We have nevertheless taken some trouble in our search for all that is interesting and genuine as concerns the Morris, in the literature of our own country, and others. For the benefit of those inclined to follow the subject farther in its historical aspect than it is herein treated, we have appended a list of books in which we have found items of interest.

So far as we can discover, there is no single work devoted to the topic: all that is to be gleaned of it from books consists only in scraps of information, most of them very brief, some contradictory; as a rule almost casually introduced in works upon dancing, ancient games and customs, and such like.

Even the origin of the name Morris and the true source of the dance are not to be traced with absolute certainty. Most authorities accept, or assert, that the dance is Moorish in origin: some again bring evidence to show that the English Morris (or Morrice) owed nothing whatever to the Moors. Still, the weight of testimony must be held to show Morocco as the fount and origin, no matter if the genius of our own folk—so very far removed from anything native to Africa—has, in the process of the centuries, altered it until it bears, in spirit, little resemblance to the parent stock.

If the spirit has been Anglicised, the steps remain. Tabourot, for instance, a very quaint and interesting writer on dancing, tells us that when he was a youth—that would be early in the 16th century—it was the custom in good society for a boy to come into the hall after supper with his face blackened, his forehead bound with white or yellow taffeta, and bells tied to his legs. He then proceeded to dance the Morisco the length of the hall, forth and back, to the great amusement of the company. So says Tabourot, long dead; and to-day we learn that, in most winters, a side of Morris-men dances at White Ladies Aston, one-and-a-half mile from Spetchley, Worcester. They blacken their faces and have for music accordion, triangle, and tambourine: their flute-player died recently. Tabourot suggests that the bells might have been borrowed from the *crotali* of the ancients in the Pyrrhic dance. He then describes the more modern Morris dance, which was performed by striking the ground with the fore part of the feet; but as this proved fatiguing the work was given to the heels, the toes being kept firm, whereby the bells jingled more effectively. He adds that this method in turn was modified, as it tended to bring on gouty complaints.

We are given by the same writer a notation of the Morisco, or Morisque, music, steps, and description: this shows as nearly as possible the steps of the Morris as we have seen it danced in England to-day.

Again, Engel, in a passage to us of extraordinary interest, gives in modern notation ". one of the tunes headed La Morisque, probably the oldest tune of the famous Morris dance still extant. As it is interesting from having been printed in the year 1550, when most likely it was already an old tune, it shall be inserted here ." And there we found the same tune which Tabourot gives for the dance that he described, as we have already told. It is the tune of "Morris Off," which we reproduce in our books of tunes. Just a few weeks earlier we had taken down, at Redditch, from the fiddler of the Bidford Morris-men, the same tune, note for note, as Tabourot gives it. Here in truth is a signal instance of that persistence and continuity which is always cropping up, to the lasting amazement and delight of the student of Folk-music—to the delight more especially of the student who, like ourselves, holds that in our Folk-music is a treasury not to be hoarded for the delectation of the scholar, but to be expended with both hands for the revivifying of a national spirit.

The Morris, then—once also the Moresc—of England; La Morisque and Morisco of France; the Moresca of Corsica, danced by armed men to represent a conflict between Moors and Christians—is in all reasonable probability Moorish in origin: never mind if in our own country it is become as English as fisticuffs, as the dance called "How d'ye do" will show—wherein our own folk, after their own manner, have suggested strife, as in the Corsican variety. Holland, as is told by Engel, was infected too; industrious research, in fact, will probably show that the Morris in some shape or other was known throughout Europe, and beyond. As for the date of its introduction into England that is impossible to state with certainty; but most authorities point to the time of Edward III., maybe when John of Gaunt returned from Spain, as probably the earliest when Morris-men were seen in England. It is said also that we had it from the French; another lays its introduction to the credit of the Flemings. The window with its Morris-men shown in our frontispiece is probably of the time of Edward IV.

Schemes of wider research, however, we are content to leave in the hands of the intrepid Folk-lorist. We are concerned here to extract from a mass of notes and references some outstanding few, to remind practising and potential Morris-dancers of to-day that this new-old art, if not indigenous, has been, like many another foreign importation, assimilated much to our advantage.

The Morisco, from which our own Morris has obviously descended, seems to have been originally both a solo and square dance, the latter being performed by sides (that is, sets) of six. The solo Morris existed all along, and still exists. When we saw our friend Kimber (mentioned elsewhere) dance his Morris jig to the tune of "Rodney," had our other old friend Tabourot been present in the spirit—maybe he was—he need have altered nothing in the description we have quoted but to substitute for the boy with his face blackened a sturdy English yeoman, and to note some differences in the get-up of the dancer. The solo dance has been performed also at Bampton, between tobacco-pipes laid crosswise on the ground—to the tune of the "Bacca Pipes" jig, or "Green Sleeves"—suggesting the Scottish sword-dance, and in many other fashions.

Another feature in the history of the English Morris, which by this time may be called impossible to account for with any exactitude, is that in the elder days the Mummers and their plays, the Robin Hood games and other ancient diversions with their characters and customs, became allied—or rather mixed up—with the Morris-men, upon May-day and occasions of festivity such as the Leet-ales, Lamb-ales, Bride-ales, &c. To what extent they were allied, or mixed, will probably baffle even the combined powers of all our archæologists to discover. In an old woodcut, for instance, preserved on the title of a penny history (Adam Bell, &c.) printed at Newcastle in 1772, is apparently the representation of a Morris dance, consisting of—A Bishop (or friar), Robin Hood, the Potter or Beggar, Little John, Friar Tuck, Maid Marian. Robin Hood and Little John carry bows of length befitting the size of each. The window, too, shown in the frontispiece is proof that the Morris-dancers were attended by other characters. The following, from Ben Jonson's "The Metamorphosed Gipsies," supplies further evidence to the same effect:—

They should be a Morris dancers by their jingle, but they have no napkins.

No, nor a hobby horse.

Oh, he's often forgotten, that's no rule; but there is no Maid Marian nor friar amongst them, which is the surer mark.

Nor a fool that I see.

But other characters, introduced for whatsoever reason, gradually disappeared, until the Morris company, as a general thing, consisted only of the dancers, the piper—that is, the musician—and the fool.

The hobby-horse, described later, was habitually associated with the Morris, until the Puritans, by their preachings and invective, succeeded in banishing it as an impious and pagan superstition. This accounts for the expression, "The hobby-horse quite forgotten"; and gives a touch of prophecy to Shakespeare's lament: "For, O, for, O, the hobby-horse is forgot." As is well known, however, the hobby-horse still prances in England to-day; at Minehead and Padstow, for instance, as an ancient and hallowed institution on its own account, and performing with the Morris-men at Bidford.

Other implements and characters may be found, used by and performing with the Morris-men, that originally had no connection with the Morris, but were borrowed from other pastimes. As we have said, however, this sets out to be no exhaustive study, whether of the Morris when it was a national dance, or of all its survivals at the present time. Such a study would in scope and purpose far outrun the limits of our intention.

Broadly speaking, the peculiar characteristics of the Morris, as it was in its heyday and as it has survived amongst us, are these: Leaving aside the solo dances, upon which we shall not touch further, the Morris is performed by six men; the records show that women have occasionally, but rarely, figured as performers. A musician is of course indispensable; also, as it seems, a fool, to supply comic relief and give the dancers breathing-time. The fool often goes by the name of "Squire," sometimes of "Rodney." These are practically invariable; but beyond and beside these, other characters have accompanied the dancers. The hobby-horse we have already mentioned as a popular addition. Some took with them an assistant, called the ragman, to carry the dancers' extra clothing. Then, a person in various disguises and habiliments went—and still goes—with the dancers to collect money, if it might be, from admiring lookers-on: sometimes the fool himself served both as the type of unwisdom and its opposite, who bears the money-box.

In some parts of the country a sword-bearer accompanied the Morris-men. This officer carried a rich pound-cake impaled upon his sword-point—cake and sword were be-ribboned, the former being supplied by some local lady; and during the dances slices of it were given amongst the audience who were expected to respond with coin for the treasury. A slice of cake was by way of bringing luck to the receiver; the credulous even treasured a piece of it the year round as a minister of good fortune.

Generally speaking, these must be regarded as the fixed and regular performers and accompaniments of the Morris. But, according to time and place, the additions to and varieties of these were innumerable. When the dance was popular, it may almost be said that every village sporting a troupe had its own peculiar variation in dress or character or other particular of its programme and *personnel*, by which it was known; and by these singularities each set of Morris-men and their backers held resolutely. There was competition, once, amongst the Morris-folk as there is to-day amongst football teams and their adherents. Many a bout, begun in friendly rivalry, ended in a scrimmage, in which the staves brought for use and ornament in the dance were used to break heads with. We are grown vastly more delicate and refined since then, it is supposed.

Before we go on to note some leading features in the dress and paraphernalia of the Morris-men, one more memory of the days that are gone—maybe in some fashion to return, maybe not—tempts to quotation. It is from the church-wardens' accounts of the parish of Kingston-upon-Thames, and in our prejudiced eyes has a dignity, and somehow a promise, all its own. It is from Lysons' "Environs of London," vol. i., 1792, p. 226, and runs:—

For paynting of the mores garments and   £ s. d.
    for sarten gret leveres
0 2 4

For 4 plyts and ½ of lawn for the mores
    garments   0 2 11

For orseden for the same
0 0 10

For bellys for the dawnsars   0 0 12

For silver paper for the mores dawnsars   0 0 7

Shoes for the mores dawnsars, the frere and
    mayde Maryan at 7d. the payre   0 5 4

8 yerds of fustyan for the mores dawnsars
    coats   0 6 0

A dosyn of gold skynnes for the morres   0 0 10

5 hats and 4 porses for the dawnsars   0 0 4½

As a conclusion to this imperfect sketch we would point once more to the warranty of its imperfections and sketchiness offered in the beginning. We hope for it no more than that it may serve to direct those inclined to bestow upon the Morris a closer study, to at least the beginnings of an enthralling subject. So much for the origin and history of the art. As for its living practitioners: of the men, for instance, of Gloucestershire, Norfolk, Lancashire, Northumberland—the last-named of whom danced the other day before the King at Alnwick Castle under the name of Guisards—and elsewhere, we offer no precise information. It may be that one day we shall be privileged to do so. But for the tunes we have set down, and for the dances belonging thereto we have attempted to describe, we do claim that in these we have tried most faithfully to pass on to others what the Morris-men gave to us.

MUSICAL INSTRUMENTS.

In earliest days of the Morris, music was made by a simple pipe, by pipe and tabour, or the bagpipe. Of these the bagpipe was apparently the original. An old madrigal, printed in 1660, runs thus:
Harke, harke, I hear the dancing
And a nimble morris prancing;
The bagpipe and the morris bells
That they are not farre hence us tells;
Come let us goe thither,
And dance like friends together.
Since the disappearance of the bagpipe, pipe and tabour (called whittle and dub) have been, even within the memory of living men, the accepted instruments wherewith to make music and beat time for the Morris. They are now fallen into disuse. The pipe or whittle was of wood, really an early form of the flageolet, over a foot long; sometimes it had a metal tongue in the mouthpiece; two finger-holes and a thumb-hole to vary the note, and was played with the left hand. From the left thumb the tabour, or dub, was suspended by a loop: the dub was a miniature drum, elaborately made, and was beaten by a stick held in the right hand. Pipe and tabour were sometimes played by separate men.

At the present time the music is generally played on a fiddle; though here, again, having no complete knowledge of all the traditional dancers still left among us, we offer no precise statement as to the instruments still in use. One Morris-man we knew made music on a concertina. *See* plate opp. p. 22 .

DRESS.

In the matter of dress, old-time accounts prove that the Morris-men indulged in considerable variety; and even amongst present-day inheritors of the tradition there are many differences. Still, certain features may be regarded as common, and the dress of Mr. Salisbury (plate opp. p. 21), leader of the Bidford men, may be cited as typical. The tall hat, though not universal, is the most popular and general headgear; and this dancer and his men wore a broad band of plaited ribbons on their hats some two-and-a-half inches wide, in red, green and white. The elaborately frilled and pleated white shirt is also typical; this was tied at wrist and elbow with blue ribbons, the ends left hanging. The breeches were of fawn-shaded corduroy, with braces of white webbing; on the braces were pinned, in front and at the back, level with the breast, rosettes of red, white and blue ribbons, the ends left hanging. The tie was of the same blue ribbon as that in the rosettes, also with the ends long and loose. The boots, as befitted the sturdy work they had to do, were substantial; the stockings of rough grey wool, which showed between the boots and breeches.

MR. SALISBURY, LEADER OF THE BIDFORD MORRIS-MEN (1906).

THE BIDFORD MORRIS SIDE.
(FIDDLER in foreground, to the right; HOBBY-HORSE—left, and FOOL—centre, beyond Dancers.)

In the case of Mr. Kimber, leader of the Headington men (plate opp. p. 22), the dress, it will be noticed, was simpler. A white sweater took the place of the pleated shirt; ribbons of red, white and blue were crossed upon the chest; the trousers were of white flannel.

Some notes on the bells and on the manner of fixing them will be found under the heading "Bells."

The fool's dress would seem to be designed to-day, as in the olden time, upon no particular plan, but to follow the fancy of the individual wearer. The Bidford man, whom we saw at his really funny antics, had a fox's mask for headgear, the muzzle lying on the man's forehead, the brush hanging down his back. His face was raddled like a clown's; he had a vest of cowhide, with red sleeves; stockings and breeches much like the dancers', and he wore his bells, not on a shin-pad like them, but in a row all round the boot-top. He carried a bladder on the end of a stick, and with it he freely whacked the hobby-horse man and occasionally members of the audience.

The hobby-horse man of the same company was dressed like a jockey; and, while the dancers had a rest, he and the fool carried on innumerable capers, sometimes backing in amongst the audience, occasionally overturning a few, and now and then chasing any maid that could be started on the run. If this pair be typical of the olden time, we can answer for it that their fun was uproarious and perfectly wholesome.

BELLS.

To the wearing of bells, stitched upon thongs and tied to the shin, there would seem to be no exception amongst the Morris-folk, even from the earliest times. The celebrated Kemp, who danced the Morris all the way from London to Norwich in 1599, and whose picture we reproduce, wore his bells in the traditional manner.

The records show that, even in recent times, both treble and tenor bells were worn, each carried by the opposite files of dancers. There are accounts also of bells with four different tones. But nowadays certainly the rule is that bells all of a kind are worn by all the dancers—latten bells, if that be still the correct name for the kind of bell to be found upon the harness that children use when they play at horses. The shin-pad that carries the bells varies to some extent in the details of its construction; the number of bells also varies. Sometimes the vertical strips and lateral ties of the pad are of ribbon or braid; maybe oftener of leather. Sometimes the bells are stitched upon the lateral ties, top and bottom; it is more usual, however, to fasten them on the perpendicular strips. The whole bell-pad is some seven inches square, and is worn midway between knee and ankle. Kimber, as will be seen (plate opposite), wears twelve bells on each leg, in three perpendicular rows of four each.

HANDKERCHIEFS.

Some dancers carry a white handkerchief—the middle finger thrust through a hole in one corner—in all their dances; we have, elsewhere, described the dances as we have seen them performed, with and without the handkerchief.

MR. KIMBER, LEADER OF THE HEADINGTON MORRIS-MEN (1906)

STICKS.

The stick, or staff, used in some dances, and the manner of using it, are described elsewhere. Sometimes a bunch of ribbons is tied to the butt; sometimes it is left unadorned.

OTHER PARAPHERNALIA.

As to the fool's properties, he always carries, after the time-honoured fashion of the clown, a bladder swinging on the end of a stick, or ladle; in some parts, even to-day, he is observing custom if he has a cow's tail on the other end: this to be used also to whack the unsuspecting looker-on.

The hobby-horse is, fundamentally, of wicker or some stout fabric stayed with wood, having a hole from which its rider, or footman, emerges to the waist, and is slung upon his shoulders in the familiar manner. The horse's head and tail, a pair of stockings stuffed and shod—and ludicrously disproportionate to the bulk of the horseman; the bit and bridle and caparison, may all be fashioned according to the horseman's humour.

"Illustrations of Shakespeare and of ancient manners." Two vols. London, 1807. Francis Douce.

"Glig-Gamena Angel-Deod, or The Sports and Pastimes of the People of England." London, 1801. Joseph Strutt.

"Observations on Popular Antiquities." Newcastle-upon-Tyne, 1777. John Brand.

"Orchesographie, et traicte en forme de dialogue, par lequel toutes personnes peuvent facilement apprendre et practiquer l'honneste exercise des dances." Lengres, 1588 (since reprinted and edited by Laure Fonta, Paris, 1888). Thoinot Arbeau (i.e., Jehan Tabourot).

"Shakespeare and his Times." Two vols. London, 1817. Dr. Nathan Drake.

"Robin Hood Ballads." London, 2nd edition, 1832. Joseph Ritson.

"The Environs of London." Four vols., 1792-96. Daniel Lysons.

"History of Music." Five vols., 1776. Reprinted, Novello, Ewer and Co., 1853, two vols. Sir John Hawkins.

"Popular Music of the Olden Time." Two vols. London, 1855-59. William Chappell.

"Shakespeare and Music." London, Dent and Co., 1896. Edward W. Naylor, M.A., Mus. Bac.

"Kemp's Nine Daies wonder, performed on a journey from London to Norwich." Edited from original. Privately printed, Edinburgh, 1884. E. Goldsmid.

"The Literature of National Music." London, Novello, Ewer and Co., 1879. Carl Engel.

"The Abbot." (Note to chap. 14.) Sir Walter Scott.

"The Fair Maid of Perth." (Note to chap. 20.) Sir Walter Scott.

"Shakespeare." (Note to Henry IV., Part I.) Steevens.

"Notes and Queries."

"Dictionary of Music and Musicians." Four vols. London, Macmillan and Co., 1879-1899. Edited by Sir George Grove.

"The Transactions of the Folk-Lore Society." Vol. 8, 1897.

"A Treatise on the art of dancing." By Giovanni-Andrea Gallini. London, 1792.

"Dancing in all Ages." London, 1879. Edward Scott.

"A Lytell geste of Robin Hode, &c." Two vols. London, Longmans, 1847.

MORRIS DANCE TUNES.

There is not much information about Morris tunes to be gathered from books. Chappell, for instance, in his "Popular Music of the Olden Time," I., pp. 125 and 130, gives but two Morris dance-tunes, "The Staines Morris Tune" and "Trip and Go"; while Mr. Edward Naylor, in the appendix to his "Shakespeare and Music," only prints the same number—"An English Morris, 1650" (a variant of Chappell's "Staines Morris Tune"), and an Italian Moresca by Claudio Monteverde, 1608. In Grove's "Dictionary of Music" (old ed.), II., p. 369, three Morris tunes are recorded: Arbeau's "Morris Off," a Yorkshire melody founded on that of "The Literary Dustman," and a Cheshire Morris to words beginning:—
Morris Dance is a very pretty tune,
I can dance in my new shoon;
In an interesting and most instructive paper on "Morris-dancing in Oxfordshire," read by Mr. Percy Manning before the Folk-Lore Society, and printed in their "Transactions" for December, 1897, five tunes are given: "Green Garters," "Constant Billy," "Willow Tree," "Maid of the Mill," and "Bob and Joan." Mr. Manning also quotes the names only of the following Morris dances and songs: "Handsome John," "Highland Mary," "Green Sleeves," "Trunk Hose," "Cockey Brown," "The Old Road," "Moll o' the Whad," "The Cuckoo," "The Cuckoo's Nest," "White Jock," and "Hey Morris." The first three of these, as well as the tunes previously mentioned, were sung or danced by the men of Bampton; the remainder by the Morris men of Field Assarts.

Our own investigations enable us to add very materially to existing knowledge of this branch of the subject. We have noted down between twenty and thirty Morris tunes, and have collected the names of several others, which no doubt we shall eventually acquire as well. The list given below consists almost entirely of tunes which are still in constant use by Morris-men in Gloucestershire, Worcestershire, Oxfordshire, and Derbyshire.

The figures in brackets record the number of times we have collected the same tune, or variants of it, from different Morris sides.
Laudnum Bunches.
Bean Setting.
Constant Billy (3).
Blue-Eyed Stranger.
The Rigs o' Marlow (2).
Old Mother Oxford.
The old Woman tossed up in a blanket (2).
Jockie to the Fair.
Rodney.
How d'ye do?
Trunkles (4).
Country Gardens.
Brighton Camp (The Girl I've left behind me) (2).
Shepherd's Hey (3).
Bluff King Hal.
We won't go home till morning.
Princess Royal (2).
Heel and Toe.
Morris Off.
Green Sleeves.
Hey Morris.
The Cuckoo's Nest.
Swag and Boney.
The Gallant Hussars.
The British Grenadiers.
The Vicar of Bray.
The Sherborne Jig.
Belle Isle's March.
Two Derbyshire tunes ("This is it, and That is it.")
It must be remembered that our investigations have up to the present been confined within a limited area, and that we have not yet attempted to deal with the northern counties of England. The experience, however, that we have already acquired is enough to prove that there are a much larger number of traditional Morris tunes still to be found in country

districts than most people would imagine. Unfortunately, many Morris sides have been disbanded within the last two or three decades, and our field of work is therefore becoming more and more restricted; for it is difficult, and in many cases impossible, to acquire accurate information unless the Morris side is actually in being. We intend, however, to continue our inquiries without pause, in order that we may collect all the existing tunes and other information upon this most interesting subject before it is too late.

We append some notes on the tunes which we are publishing in connection with this volume, with the exception of "Bean Setting," "Trunkles," and "Laudnum Bunches," about which we know nothing.

NOTES ON MORRIS TUNES.

"HOW D'YE DO?"

Compare "Blowzabella, my bouncing Doxie," in d'Urfey's "Pills to purge melancholy," I., p. 190 (Ed. 1719).

"RIGS O' MARLOW."

This air is printed in Burke Thumoth's collection of Irish Airs (1720), in Holden's "Old Irish Tunes" (1806), and in "Songs of Ireland," p. 164 (Boosey).

T. Crofton Croker quotes the words of the original song in "The Popular Songs of Ireland" (1839), of which the first verse is as follows:—
AIR—"Sandy lent the man his Mull."
Beauing, belling, dancing, drinking,
Breaking windows, damning, sinking,
Ever raking, never thinking,
Live the rakes of Mallow.
Mr. Kimber, the leader of the Headington Morris, could only give us the first verse of their song, which, however, is quite different from the Irish words:—
When I go to Marlow Fair
With the ribbons in my hair,
All the boys and girls declare,
Here comes the rigs o' Marlow.
Mallow is in County Cork and was a fashionable watering-place in the eighteenth century, when it was known as the "Irish Bath." Croker says that the young men of that fashionable watering-drinking town were proverbially called "the rakes of Mallow," and he adds: "A set of pretty pickles they were, if the song descriptive of their mode of life, here recorded after the most delicate oral testimony, is not very much over-coloured."

Neither the Oxfordshire nor the Gloucestershire Morris-men, from both of whom we recovered this tune, had probably heard of "Mallow"; it was natural enough, therefore, to substitute "Marlow," which, of course, they know very well.

"COUNTRY GARDENS."

This is the prototype of "The Vicar of Bray," and Mr. Kidson tells us that he has it in an old book of airs under the more ancient title. It is also called "The Country Garden" in Playford's "Dancing Master," and in Chappell's "National English Airs," Nos. 25 and 26. Chappell gives it in 3-4 time, and remarks that it then becomes "a plaintive love ditty instead of a sturdy and bold air."

"SHEPHERD'S HEY."

This air bears some resemblance to "The Faithful Shepherd" in Thompson's "Complete Collection of Country Dances" (*circa* 1775), which is reprinted in Mr. Kidson's "Old English Country Dances," p. 10.

"CONSTANT BILLY."

This is a variant of the "Constant Billy" printed in Playford's "Dancing Master" (1726), p. 170, and also in one of Walsh's dancing books. It is also in Gay's "Beggars' Opera," where it is set to the words, "Cease your funning." Mr. Kidson tells us that the air is known in old books as "Over hills and lofty mountains" or "Lofty mountains."

The well-known Welsh air "The Ash Grove" is but another version of the same tune; but whether the Welsh derived the air from England or *vice versa* is a moot point. The matter is discussed, at some length, in Chappell's "Popular Music of the Olden Time," p. 665, to which the reader is referred.

The air that we print is as the Headington Morris-men played it; but we also recovered a variant of it from the Bidford dancers. The "Constant Billy" of the Bampton men, already mentioned, is yet another variant, but in the Æolian mode.

The words of the first verse of the Headington version were as follows:
O Constant Billy,
Shall I go with 'ee?
O when shall I see
My Billy again?
The Bampton words were different:
O my Billy, my constant Billy,
When shall I see my Billy again?
When the fishes flies over the mountains
Then you will see your Billy again.

"BLUE-EYED STRANGER."

Mr. Kidson tells us that this is a variant of "The Mill, Mill, O" in "Orpheus Caledonius," I., p. 40 (1725). It has also some points in common with "Just as the tide was a-flowing" in "Folk-Songs from Somerset," II., No. 37 (and note).

"BLUFF KING HAL."

This is a version in the major mode of "The Staines Morris Tune," published in the first edition of Playford's "Dancing Master," and reprinted in Chappell's "Popular Music of the Olden Time," I. , p. 126. How it has come to be christened "Bluff King Hal" we do not know unless, as Mr. Kidson suggests, the Bidford Morris men have taken the name from some modern collection of old English dances.

"MORRIS OFF."

As has already been stated, this tune, which was given us by the Bidford Morris dancers, is printed in Thoinot Arbeau's "Orchesographie," p. 94. A Dutch version of the same air is included in a collection of dance-tunes by Tielman Susato (Antwerp, 1551); and is reprinted in Carl Engel's "Literature of National Music," p. 56. See also Grove's "Dictionary of Music" (old ed.) II., 369.

THE DANCE.

The Morris Dance is essentially a manifestation of vigour rather than of grace. This is probably true of all country dances: it is pre-eminently true of the Morris dance. It is, in spirit, the organized, traditional expression of virility, sound health and animal spirits. It smacks of cudgel-play, of quarter-staff, of wrestling, of honest fisticuffs. There is nothing sinuous in it, nothing dreamy; nothing whatever is left to the imagination. It is a formula based upon and arising out of the life of man, as it is lived by men who hold much speculation upon the mystery of our whence and whither to be unprofitable; by men of meagre fancy, but of great kindness to the weak: by men who fight their quarrels on the spot with naked hands, drink together when the fight is done, and forget it, or, if they remember, then the memory is a friendly one. It is the dance of folk who are slow to anger, but of great obstinacy—forthright of act and speech: to watch it in its thumping sturdiness is to hold such things as poinards and stilettos, the swordsman with the domino, the man who stabs in the back—as unimaginable things.

The Morris dance, in short, is a perfect expression in rhythm and movement of the English character.

THE MORRIS STEP.

As we have told already, the Morris dance is a bodily manifestation of vigour and rude health, and not at all of sinuous grace or dreaminess. This will be obvious at a glance to anyone who watches the traditional Morris dancer at his evolutions. The first step, therefore, towards acquiring the true art of the Morris-man is to put away all thought and remembrance of the ballroom manner—really to unlearn, so far as possible, the lessons of the dancing-master and all his exhortations upon and exhibitions of glide, pirouette, *chassez*; the pointed toe, the gently swaying body, the elegant waving and posturing such as become the finished performer of round and square dances in the drawing-room. To say, put away for a while these methods is to put no slight upon them, or to offer a word of criticism: it is requisite and necessary, even as one should advise a change of clothing to somebody about to quit the ballroom for some rough-and-tumble pastime in the open fields.

Firstly, as to the manner of the steps. The Morris-men wear bells strapped to their shins; the bells are there that they may ring their music—and a fine wholesome music it is, too: to ring, they must be well shaken; to be shaken, the leg they are strapped to must be kicked and stamped. Get that principle into your head, and that practice into your legs, and you make the first long stride towards acquisition of the art of Morris dancing. Strap a set of bells to your shins, get out upon a grass-plot or the King's highway; never mind elegance or the criticism of the emasculate modern: kick and stamp upon the earth in such a manner as to make your bells ring their loudest, and ring all together. You will see pretty soon that, to do so, you must, when you jump, let the heels come solidly to earth, immediately following the toes—no man, even an old-time Morris-man, may jump and alight upon his heels alone, with the spine held rigidly above them (*see* p. 33). You will find also that, in stepping it, whether to advance or retire, or to step rhythmically in one place, to make your bells ring the true *fortissimo* you must *kick*, and kick hard.

Half an hour's experiment of this kind will do more to instil into the would-be dancer the spirit that presides at Morris revels than chapters of exhortation. It is a robust and friendly spirit, and will set the learner's steps—given that he be of English blood, or even of Anglo-Saxon sympathy—a-thumping to its solid downrightness.

Once possessed of the spirit, the form of the Morris step needs little explanation and description, for the steps are few and simple. With an eye upon the foregoing notes and, it is hoped, a personal memory of the experiment as recommended, the learner will readily grasp the description that follows here.

Roughly, the Morris step is alike throughout all the dances; it varies only in force, length (i.e., the length of the stride varies more or less), and height (i. e., the foot is lifted more or less).

The foot, when lifted, is never drawn back, but always thrust forward. The toe is never pointed in line with the leg, but held at a right-angle to it, as in the standing position. The foot, therefore, the forward or stepping foot, is lifted as in walking, as if to step forward, then the leg is vigorously straightened to a kick, so as to make the bells ring. At the same instant that the forward leg is straightened, a hop is made on the rear foot; the dancer alights upon the toe, but lets the heel follow immediately and firmly, so that he stands upon the flat foot. A good snap-shot photograph of one in the act of walking, when the forward foot has made about three-fourths of its stride, gives a perfect illustration of the Morris dancer's step.

As with the step, so also with the jump, which in so many cases begins and ends a measure; the dancer jumps, roughly, as high as his own foot, holding when in air legs and body straight, alighting upon the toes, but only so as to break the shock sufficiently for comfort, then letting the heels come firmly down. In alighting from the jump, the knees are bent just enough to save the dancer from injurious shock, and are straightened immediately.

Such are the Morris step and jump; the jump never varies; the step does vary as to height, length and vigour of stride, as will presently be noted. It must, however, constantly be borne in mind that, high or low, there is always sturdiness in the Morris step; to Morris-men the languorous and the lackadaisical are for ever unknown.

For the purposes of compiling a notation, we have classified the steps necessary to the dances described into two, as follows:—

In the step most commonly used the raised foot is thrust forward only so far that, when the leg is straightened to the kick, the forward heel is roughly the length of the dancer's foot in advance of the toe of the rear or supporting foot. This step, it must be remembered, will be used always, except when specific instructions are given to make it higher or lower.

In the high step, used chiefly in the figures called "Capers" (*see* p. 50), the dancer must, if his activity will allow of it, raise the forward foot until its toe is as high as the knee of the rear or supporting leg. It is an exercise not to be attempted all at once in its completeness, because it is one well calculated to send the inexperienced enthusiast sprawling on his back. Its study should be approached gently, by way of familiarity with the simpler movement, which, once it is mastered, may easily be extended to the harder one. The latter must be approached with caution—that is all. And the novice is to bear constantly in mind that, in the matter of vigour, he simply cannot put too much of it into his Capers. There will be little trouble about his remembering that, however; the Morris Caper-music will not let him forget it for a moment.

This step is called in the Notation—High.

It has always to be remembered that in Morris dancing, unless definite instructions be given to the contrary, every movement or part of a movement is begun by stepping out with the right foot.

DIAGRAMS OF MORRIS STEPS.

WITH NOTATION MARKS ADDED.

Steps used in 4-time music (whether simple or compound). The letters R and L signify right or left foot.

This is called in the Notation—4/1.
This is called in the Notation—4/2.
This is called in the Notation—4/3.
This is called in the Notation—4/4.

STEPS USED IN 6-TIME (i.e., COMPOUND 2).

WITH NOTATION MARKS ADDED.

This is called in the Notation—6/1.

This is called in the Notation—6/2.

This is called in the Notation—6/3.

These steps are perfectly simple, and all but one may be learned at a glance, even by one who has no knowledge of music, for such a one has only to keep his eye upon the beats, which give the rhythm.

The exception—the only one that presents a difficulty at first—is the one marked 4/3 and 6/3, these two being one, since only the time differs; the feet step the same in each. A hint will make this step come as easily as the rest. Let the beginner in temporary difficulty with it bethink himself of the polka-step; sing a stave of the polka, and dance round the room to it. He will find that his feet are stepping exactly in order of the Morris 4/3 and 6/3 step—left, right, left, hop-left; right, left, right, hop-right, and so on. Now, all he has to do in order to adapt the polka to the Morris four-time step of 4/3 is, firstly to manage his feet as described, then to make the hop at end of each bar of the polka not as it were a dotted note, but in even measure with the other beats: for the last step of each bar to Morris four-time music is a hop, as in the polka, but in even time and in the Morris fashion.

Now, having adapted the polka step to the Morris 4/3, let the learner simply count six to the bar and step to it in exactly the same way. He will find, given just an average ear for rhythm, that he will soon be dancing thus, counting as he

       1 2 3   4 5 6
dances--1, 2, 3, 4, 5, 6--Right--left, Right--right;
   1 2 3   4 5 6
Left--right, Left--left.

Having mastered these, one last instruction may be given. The 4/3 Morris step is occasionally varied, so as to make it exactly like the polka-step—that is, with the final hop danced like a dotted note; like a quaver, if the music be in common time. This is a variation practised occasionally by the Morris men themselves, and the enthusiastic amateur will find himself dropping into it occasionally, following his enthusiastic leader. No instructions for this changing of the step will be given in the Notation, for it cannot be specified. The whole side will fall into it naturally, upon occasion: for instance, where there is a long stretch of the step, danced in one position, couples facing, arms swinging and handkerchiefs waving, as in "Blue-eyed Stranger." This is fairly intoxicating to the dancer, and here the hop will often suggest itself. And again, in hurrying, if one gets left behind a pace, as, for instance, in the Chain. But to hop, or not to hop, unevenly in the 4/3 step, that is a matter that will be easily arranged by the spirit of the dancers and the discretion of their leader. We desire merely to indicate a rule that, upon occasion, may be agreeably infringed.

POSITIONS, AND CHANGE OF POSITION.

The Morris side, when in position for dancing, stands in, or returns to, the positions as shown hereunder. The only exception to these is the Ring, as explained below.

POSITION 1 (COLUMN).
POSITION 2 (Front).

1 2   1>

Thus the six stand in two parallel lines of three each. The top, as the rule is in dancing, is set towards the music. The angles represent the dancers: the apex of each angle points as the dancer's face is turned; the numbers within the angles will be used throughout in describing movements of individual dancers.

The dancer at the top left-hand

corner, No. 1, is *invariably* the leader of the side. No figure is completed, and no dance can end, until No. 1 has returned to his place at the top left-hand corner.

It is the duty and privilege of No. 1 to call loudly and clearly the name of each figure or part of a figure as each falls due for performance—"Corners," "Chain," "Back-to-back," and so forth, and to announce the end of the dance by the call of "All in."

In Position 1, or Column, the dancers stand in two files, and all face the same way.

This is called in the Notation—Column, or Col.

In Position 2, or Front, the dancers are turned inward, and face each other in pairs.

This is called in the Notation—Front, or Fr.

The change of position, from Column to Front, or *vice versa*, whether made by jumping or by stepping to measure, is executed invariably thus:—

To change Column to Front the dancers turn inward. Thus, in Position 1, Nos. 1, 3, and 5 make a half-turn to the right; Nos. 2, 4, and 6 make a half-turn to the left.

To change Front to Column, in Position 2, Nos. 1, 3, and 5 will make a half-turn to the left; Nos. 2, 4, and 6 a half-turn to the right.

In changing from Column to Front when the column is reversed—that is, the dancers having their backs to the music—the half-turns as given above will be reversed also.

As for the distance to be maintained between individual dancers, whether in Column or Front, the files (i.e., odd and even numbers) should stand so far apart that, when arms are extended, the hands of each will overlap his neighbour's hands.

The distance between the files will vary according to the nature of the dance. In the Stick and Handkerchief dances, pairs (Nos. 1 and 2, &c.) stand near enough to clap hands or tap sticks with each other. In the Corner dances, as will readily be seen from the descriptions and Notation, the files must be well apart to give plenty of room for the necessary movements. The right distance will easily be found; roughly, the side should form a square measuring some twelve feet each way.

In the Notation, the term "Partners" is used to denote the pairs as they stand fronting or abreast, Nos. 1 and 2, 3 and 4, 5 and 6.

The term "Opposites" is used in referring to couples when they must change places, or re-change, as in Corners and Capers, Nos. 1 and 6, 2 and 5, 3 and 4. The latter couple, the centres, it will be noticed, will have both terms applied to them, according as the movement described is Corners or Capers, or another, such as hand-striking.

In some dances, as, for instance, in "Bean-setting," the side forms a ring, and many dances end in this formation. Instructions for this, as and where it occurs, will be found in the Notation, and will be marked under Formation, thus:—Ring.

EVOLUTIONS.

Here follows a detailed description, with diagrams, of the various evolutions necessary to the dances which we have embodied in this series; to each evolution a Notation word is attached.

The best way for a teacher who has never seen the dances performed, yet wants to teach them from the book, is to study the diagrams and learn by heart the Notation word for each. He should then stand a side upon the floor, make them go through the evolutions by word of command, or Notation word, slowly, as described; counting the beats, but without music.

This manner of beginning is advised only when the teacher has nothing but the book for guide: where an experienced dancer is available we have found it best for the novices to set to at once upon the dance; the practised one showing steps, evolutions, &c, as they occur.

DOWN-AND-BACK; AND UP-AND-BACK.

This movement occurs at the beginning of so many dances that to simplify matters it will be described here, and symbols will be attached to the description and used in the Notation. The movement is executed as follows:

The side stands in Column, and starts by advancing for the first two bars, and retiring for the second two bars. Each file advances and retires its own length; that is, Nos. 1 and 2 will move ahead, the others following, until Nos. 3 and 6 have come to the places of Nos. 1 and 2; in the next two bars all get back to position.

The two bars' advance is made always according to the time of the music, either at 4/3 or 6/3 step: the two bars' retiring is always made at 4/2 or 6/2 step (*see* p. 48).

The whole movement is made in eight bars. In one dance, the second four bars are danced the same way as the first four; but in all the others the Column is reversed at the end of the first four bars. The two ways of executing the movement will be marked in the Notation as follows:

When the side is to advance and retire twice, without reversing at end of fourth bar, and is to form Front at the end of bar 8, this will be marked in the Notation, so:

MUSIC.   MOVEMENTS.   FORMA'
A.   Down-and-back   Col. to Fr.
         twice, then j.
         (Forming Fr.)

When the side is to advance and retire, reversing position at beginning of fifth bar, and in bars 5 to 8 facing the opposite way, then at end of bar 8 forming Front, this will be found marked in the Notation, so:

MUSIC.   MOVEMENTS.   FORMA'
A.   Down-and-   Column.
         back, Ju.
         Up-and-back, j.   Col. to Fr.
         (forming Fr.)

THE CHAIN.

This movement is also completed in eight bars.

In the following diagram (Figs. 1, 2, and 3) the movements of the leading three, Nos. 1, 3, and 5, are shown separately to avoid confusion.

To begin the Chain the side stands in Column (*see* p. 48). No. 1 turns *outward*, that is, to the left, and goes forward in an S-shaped double curve as shown, passing in the middle of the curve the place of No. 3, and finishing in the place of No. 5.

No. 3 starts out to rightward, and goes in a circle, in the second half of which he is following the first half of No. 1's track.

No. 5 starts to leftward, making a double curve as No. 1, but opposite, passing in the middle of it the place of No. 3, and finishing in the place of No. 1.

Fig. 1., Fig. 2. & Fig. 3.

Therefore, No. 8 follows No. 1, and No. 5 follows No. 3 round the track of an imaginary figure 8, or double circle, for that is the shape of the completed movement. Thus:

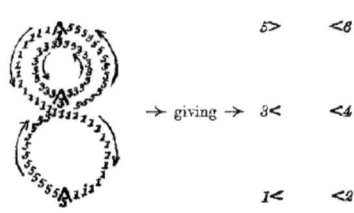

Fig. 4. & Fig. 5.

[NOTE.—At middle and completion of Chain, all turn inward, as shown in Fig. 5, and face partners as they jump (*see* p. 48).]

At the end of the second bar, No. 5 should be at No. 3's place, in the centre of the figure; No. 1 should have already passed it, and No. 3 be coming to it, so that No. 5 passes between Nos. 1 and 3. In second half of Chain, same positions are to be observed.

In the second four bars, for completion of the Chain, the movements already described are simply reversed. As No. 1 is always leader (*see*

38), and must turn outward and be followed by Nos. 3 and 5 on the lines of the figure 8, he must now return to his station along the double curve travelled in the first four bars by No. 5. No. 3 must follow No. 1 in the other circle of the 8, and No. 5 must get back to his station along the double curve travelled in the first four bars by No. 1. Thus:

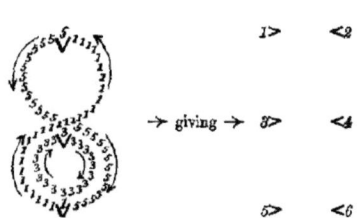

Fig. 6. & Fig. 7.

The Chain is danced by Nos. 2, 4, and 6 precisely in the same way: No. 2 is always leader; always turns *outward*; and Nos. 4 and 6 always follow No. 2 on the lines of the double curve, or figure 8. No. 6, as No. 5, passes between Nos. 2 and 4, in chaining.

Occasionally, as for instance in "Country Gardens," the term "Half-chain" will be found. This means that the movement shown in Fig. 4 is executed to four bars of music; another movement follows; then "Half-chain" again, bringing numbers back to original stations.

If, as very often occurs, the Chain follows a movement executed in Front formation, the dancers simply turn and follow one another as shown in diagrams, when the Chain music begins.

This is called in the Notation—Chain.

CROSS-OVER.

This movement is executed in Front formation, to eight bars of music, as follows:

In the first two bars each dancer crosses over and takes the place of his partner, setting the pairs back to back, thus:

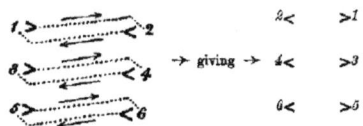

Fig. 1. & Fig. 2.

In crossing and re-crossing, *invariably*, each must keep his partner to
the right, that is, the right shoulder of each passes by the right
shoulder of each partner.

In bars 3 and 4 (keeping up the step all the time) all come to the
right-about, that is, face inward again, by turning to the rightward
(maintaining position all the time), thus:

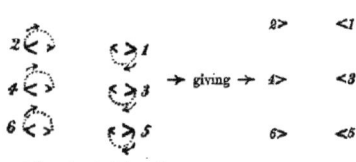

Fig. 4. & Fig. 5.

In bars 5 and 6 all cross over again, right shoulder to right shoulder,
bringing the side back to back and in original stations.

In bars 7 and 8 all make a full turn to the right (as in Fig. 3) bringing
the side again to Front.

As there are two bars to turn in after crossing over, and again after
re-crossing, the dancer must, of course, turn slowly and evenly, so that
the turn is completed just in time for the jump in bars 4 and 8.

This is called in the Notation—Cross-over.

BACK-TO-BACK.

As with the Cross-over, this movement is completed in eight bars.

In the first four bars partners advance, right shoulder to right
shoulder, but not touching, pass one another, move to the right, re-pass
partners (left shoulder to left shoulder), and retire to position, moving
backwards. Thus:

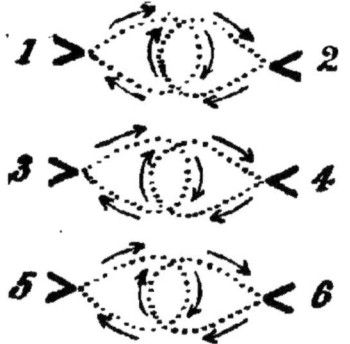

Fig. 1.

In bars 4 to 8 partners advance, left shoulder to left shoulder, pass,
move to the left, retire backwards, re-passing right shoulder to right
shoulder, and so to original station. Thus:

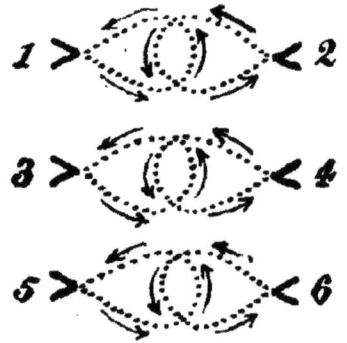

Fig. 2.

This is called in the Notation—Back-to-back.

GO-AND-COME.

This is a form of the Cross-over, but made without turning. It is
executed in Front formation, to eight bars of music. In the first two
bars partners cross exactly as in the Cross-over—right shoulder to right
shoulder. In bars 3 and 4, instead of turning, retire backwards in the
line they crossed—right shoulder to right shoulder. In bars 5 and 6 they
cross again, but left shoulder to left shoulder, and in bars 7 and 8
retire on the same line—left to left again.

This is called in the Notation—Go-and-Come.

THE RING.

In this, wherever it occurs, partners simply alter positions so that the
whole side forms a ring, or circle. It is sometimes used at the finish of
a dance; and in "Bean-setting" it occurs at the beginning. (*See*
diagrams, p. 51.)

This is called in the Notation—Ring.

STEPS IN FOREGOING EVOLUTIONS.

Unless special instructions are given to the contrary, the step used in
bars 1 and 2 of "Chain," "Cross-over," "Back-to-back" and "Go-and-come,"
is always 4/3 or 6/3, according to time, and 4/2 or 6/2 in bars 3 and 4;
likewise, 4/3 or 6/3 in bars 5 and 6, and 4/2 or 6/2 in bars 7 and 8.

THE JUMP.

The manner of the Jump has been described already (*see* p. 33). It remains to tell of the different ways in which the movement is employed, and to assign to each a Notation number.

The Jump is used in two ways only, as follows:—

1. In position. That is, the dancer jumps where he stands, without changing front.

This is called in the Notation—Ju.

2. To make a half-turn. That is, in military phrase, to make a "half-right—or left—turn."

This is called in the Notation—j.

For direction—to left or right—of turning, *see* instructions under "Positions, and change of position."

The following rules as to the Jump apply to Handkerchief and Corner dances, and are invariable. In Stick dances tapping to a great extent takes the place of jumping, but in these, where the Jump is to be used, it will be found marked in the Notation. Movements of the hands, which invariably go with the Jump, will be found under heading "The Hands."

The first general rule is this: Every dancer whose turn it is to execute any movement whatsoever, must jump on last half-bar before that movement begins. This applies, as the case may be, to the whole side, or to any pair of opposites about to execute any figure or movement.

For instance, the whole side is to dance Down-and-back and Up-and-back, so on last half-bar of "Once to Yourself," the whole side jumps together—then starts the figure. Also in all figures executed by the whole side in common—in "Chain," "Cross-over," "Back-to-back," "Go-and-come"—all jump together on last half-bar before the figure begins.

It is the same with pairs or opposites. In Corners and Capers each pair whose turn it is to dance together jump on last half-bar before they begin. As each pair finishes the next must be ready to jump on last half-bar before their turn. So with the third pair; and as they finish, and the whole side takes up the next figure in common, then the whole side jumps together on last half-bar.

So much for the Jump as an invariable preliminary to all figures in the Stick and Handkerchief dances. We come now to the Jump as made at the middle and end of figures.

In the first place there are the figures executed by the whole side in common.

All, then, having jumped on last half-bar before the figure is begun, jump also at middle and end of the figure as follows:—

In "Down-and-back," Ju., "Up-and-back," j. (forming Fr.), *see* Notation , the side goes forward and back as described (*see* p. 40) for four bars; jumps together on half-bar of bar 4, still facing in the same direction. That completes "Down-and-back," Ju. Then, instantly, they all make a complete turn to the right—right-about—dance as before in bars 5 to 8, and on last half-bar of bar 8 all jump, and as they jump make a half-turn inward. That completes "Up-and-back," j. (forming Fr.).

The Chain, though it is executed in Column formation, follows upon a figure executed in Front. So the preliminary jump, before beginning Chain, is made Front; files make half-Chain, end numbers change places, and at half-bar of bar 4, all jump, j., in a half-turn to Front; then complete Chain and jump to Front again, j., on last half-bar of bar 8.

In "Cross-over," "Back-to-back," "Go-and-come," all executed in Front formation, the whole side jumps in position, Ju., at half-bar in bars 4 and 8.

In Corners and Capers, *wherever opposites change places*, the rule is that they jump on last half-bar, as they finish their part in the figure—that is, as they complete the movement of changing or re-changing places.

In "Blue-eyed Stranger," where the whole side dances in position for eight bars, all jump at half-bar in bar 8. Should the side elect to keep up the step for sixteen bars (*see* p. 50), then all jump at half-bar in bar 16.

In "Bluff King Hal" and "Morris Off," there is no Jump at all.

THE HANDS.

The movements of the hands are made invariably according to rule, as follows:—

These rules apply, as with the Jump, to all Handkerchief and Corner dances.

In making the Jump, the hands are always, with rigid arms, thrown above the head.

In "Down-and-back" and "Up-and-back," "Chain," "Cross-over," "Back-to-back," "Go-and-come," movements of the hands are always the same. That is: Commencing with the preliminary Jump, when the hands are above the head, on beginning of first bar, with first step (of 4/3 or 6/3 step), hands are swung backward; forward on half-bar; back again, beginning of bar 2, and forward on half-bar of bar 2. In bar 3 (4/2 or

6/2 step) the hands, being already upward and forward, are swung twice in
a circle, commencing inward, so that the handkerchiefs are waved in a double circle over the head. At beginning of bar 4 the hands are lowered
straight in line with the body, and at half-bar of bar 4, with the Jump, they are thrown straight above the head on rigid arms.

These movements of the hands are always the same in every Handkerchief and Corner dance. Whenever the 4/3 or 6/3 step is used the hands are swung as already described. Also, wherever there are the two bars of 4/2 or 6/2 step, the hands are also used as already described—double circle overhead; down, and up on the Jump.

In Capers, wherever the 4/1 or 6/1 High Step is used, the hands are swung backward on beginning of bar, forward and upward on half-bar; and this movement is continued all the time the High Step (4/1 or 6/1) is used.

The arms in all these movements described, should really be swung as far,
both backward and forward, as possible. The Morris-men themselves swing
the arms behind to an angle of 45 degrees or so; but in the forward swing their hands are raised forward and a little higher than the head, on arms slightly bent at the elbows.

THE CALL.

In the Notation it will be seen that at the end of some dances the side is instructed to "Call." This means that on last half-bar all raise their voices on a high-note "Ah!" something after the manner of Scottish dancers, though the Morris "Call" is less of a war-whoop and more of a lusty shout.

LENGTH OF DANCES.

It must always be remembered that the Morris-men themselves vary the length of their dances, according to the humour of the moment, and their freshness or fatigue. A dance can always be shortened by leaving out one or more figures: the musician will know what to do by the call of the leader.

In "Blue-eyed Stranger," for instance, if the side is feeling particularly high-spirited, the whole sixteen bars of "B" music may be danced; but as a rule this will be found too long. Again, to extend "Rigs o' Marlow" (another trying dance) the music may be played four times instead of three, when Back-to-back will be danced to "A" music. "Bluff King Hal," danced to its full length as shown in the Notation, will as a general rule also be found too long. It can easily be shortened by leaving out repetitions or certain figures. In brief, once the dances are learned it is a very simple matter, and quite according to tradition, to lengthen or abbreviate them in any way desired.

SPECIAL INSTRUCTIONS FOR VARIOUS DANCES.

BEAN-SETTING (STICK DANCE).

TO FORM RING.

This is the only one of those dances we have described that begins with the Ring. The side starts in Column. To form Ring, Nos. 3 and 4 move a little outward from the line as "A" music begins. Then all dance in Ring formation to the right (*see* Fig. 1) until, at the beginning of bar 4,
all opposites have changed places: that is, Nos. 1 and 6 are each in the other's position, Nos. 3 and 4, 2 and 5

have also changed. In bar 4,
files close in slightly, j. (*i.e.*, form Column), and tap sticks across
on half-bar of bar 4. In remaining four bars of "A" music form Ring
again, and all return to position as they came (*see* Fig. 2). At
half-bar in bar 8, all j. (forming Column), and partners tap sticks across.

Fig. 1.

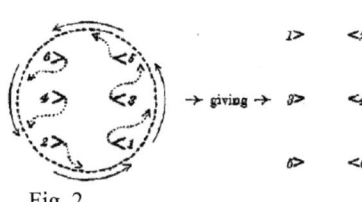

Fig. 2.

DIBBING.

This is the term used in the dance, as it is used in field and garden
work, for making a hole with a dib, or dibber, in the soil, into which
the seed is dropped. The dance, of course, represents the setting of
beans—more truly and largely, the sowing of the seed in springtime.

In dibbing (*see* □ in music) all stoop well forward, holding the
right hands outward, with sticks pointing to the ground. The act of
dibbing consists in thumping the stick firmly on the floor and at once
lifting it again.

B.

Bar 1.—Dib all together at beginning and half-bar, as shown in music
(□).

Bar 2.—Remain stooped; at beginning of bar, pairs tap sticks across—odd numbers tapping even numbers. Hold sticks crossed as they were tapped for remainder of bar.

Bar 3.—Dibbing, as in bar 1.

Bar 4.—Beginning, partners tap across; half-bar, No. 1 taps No. 3.

Bar 5.—Beginning, No. 3 taps No. 5; half-bar, No. 5 taps No. 6.

Bar 6 (9/8 time).—Beginning, No. 6 taps No. 4; second beat, No. 4 taps No. 2; third beat, partners tap across, as in bar 2.

In remaining six bars of "B," repeat dibbing and tapping as in the first six bars.

In the notation of "Bean-setting" (p. 61), the term "Dibbing" will be used to denote all the actions, here explained in detail, that go to the music of "B."

COUNTRY GARDENS (HANDKERCHIEF DANCE).

In the hand-striking figure of this dance (for hand-strokes, *see* mark O in "B" music) there are four movements, as follows:—

Each dancer strikes both hands together. This is called in the
   Notation that follows—b.

   Each, with the right hand, strikes the right hand of partner.
     This is marked in the Notation—r.

   Each, with the left hand, strikes the left hand of partner. This
    is marked in Notation—l.

   Each throws up hands. This is marked in Notation—u.

In striking, handkerchiefs are held bunched together in the hands.

NOTATION OF HAND-STRIKING.

CONSTANT BILLY (STICK DANCE).

In this, sticks are held and used, both in the "A" and "B" music, as explained in "Rigs o' Marlow" (*see* p. 55).

Stick-tapping in "B" music is done according to the following diagram: signs, &c., to be read as in diagrams for "Rigs o' Marlow" (*see* X in music). The beats whereon stick-tappings occur are written in diagram as b. (bar); and h.-b. (half-bar).

In the first bar of "B" music, at half-bar, No. 1, with top end, taps butt of No. 2. In the second bar, at half-bar, No. 2, with top end, taps butt of No. 1. In the third bar, at half-bar, No. 1 taps No. 2 as in first bar. In the fourth bar, No. 1, at the beginning, with the butt, taps No. 2's top end; and at half-bar, No. 1, with top, taps top end of No. 2, thus:—

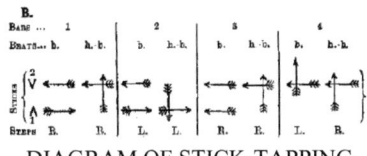

DIAGRAM OF STICK-TAPPING.

The steps are the same for all. When tapping is continued (*see* Notation) for eight bars, then, in the last four, all start on the left foot, and step thus: L.L.R.R.L.L.R.L. Tapping is the same in first and second four bars.

In tapping, of course, odd numbers do as No. 1 in diagram, even numbers as No. 2.

RIGS O' MARLOW (STICK DANCE).

In this the sticks are held throughout by the middle, in the manner explained (*see* p. 60). In all single-tapping passages, to "A" music, sticks are held slanting upward, like a single-stick, but with the upper arm close to the body. In Column formation, odd numbers—that is, leading file—hold the forearm to rightward; even numbers—right file—hold the forearm across the body, so that the sticks cross between files, ready for tapping. Leading file always taps the other file, which holds the sticks firm.

In the double-tapping, to "B" music, sticks are held in the middle, hand below stick, which is now held straight, parallel with the ground, advanced towards partner, and raised about as high as the neck.

The following diagram will show how sticks are tapped in this movement.
Angles and numbers, as in p. 54, &c., represent the leader and partner, Nos. 1 and 2: the other pairs, of course, tap precisely as these two, odd and even numbers respectively.

The arrows between angles represent sticks. As tapping has now to be done
with both ends of the sticks, these are shown in this way. The barbed end is the top, the feather the butt-end. The top is held always to the right—butt, or barb, to leftward of

each dancer. The tapping will be shown bar by bar. The steps shown apply to *all* the dancers.

In the first bar of "B" music, No. 1, with top end, taps the butt of No. 2, on beats 3 and 4, thus:—

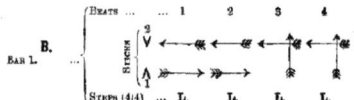

DIAGRAM OF STICK-TAPPING.

In the second bar of "B" music, No. 2, with top end, taps the butt of No. 1, on beats 3 and 4, thus:—

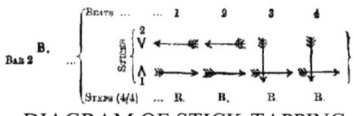

DIAGRAM OF STICK-TAPPING.

In the third bar of "B" music, No. 1 taps No. 2 precisely as in bar 1. Same step.

In the fourth bar of "B" music, No. 1 taps No. 2 on every beat, as follows:

First beat, No. 1, with butt end, taps No. 2 on top end.

Second beat, with top end, taps butt.

Third beat, with butt, taps top.

Fourth beat, with top end, taps top of No. 2.

Thus:—

DIAGRAM OF STICK-TAPPING.
DIAGRAM OF STICK-TAPPING.

This double-tapping looks complicated, both in dance and diagram, but is
really very simple. A few hints upon the most difficult bar, the fourth, will explain the whole. In this, on beat 1, No. 1, to tap with his butt the top of No. 2's stick, raises the wrist and hand till the stick is above and at right-angles to No. 2's, then thrusts outward till his butt strikes No. 2's top. On beat 2, No. 1 lowers his hand, keeping the stick perpendicular, moves hand to right and taps his top on No. 2's butt. Beat 3 is as beat 1; on beat 4, No. 1 simply lowers hand and taps No. 2 on his right, or top end. This explains all the taps that occur.

For the method, which is invariable, except where specially stated, of holding the stick (*see* p. 60).

In the second four bars of "B," double-tapping and steps are repeated precisely as in first four bars; and throughout the dance it is the same to "B" music, four bars of double-tapping, repeated, up to the call "All in."

BLUFF KING HAL.

In this the step is 4/3 throughout. It should be danced something after the fashion of "Morris-Off," but not quite so soberly; yet the step is less vigorous than the normal Morris step. Like "Morris-Off" it has, what with its length and staid monotony, a quaintness all its own. To teach and to learn the right way of dancing "Bluff King Hal" is more a matter of drill and precision than lusty *abandon*: it must be danced evenly, seriously almost, and quite quietly, or its true effect will be marred or lost.

The music is marked *ad libitum*: the musician simply brings his labours to an end in whichsoever section he shall hear the warning call of "All in." Even the Morris-men themselves do not invariably go through all the movements. These instructions are given in order that, should audience or dancers weary of the exercise, it can be curtailed. Where we have taught the dance to novices, we have found, at first, curtailment to be advisable, for the length and monotony of it palled. Later, however, when the learners had mastered its curious intricacies, we found no weariness amongst them, but a constant demand for every single movement to be performed in its traditional completeness, and over and over again, as
long as we chose to play it. We shall therefore describe it here at length, and leave it to the tact and discretion of the teacher where and when and to what extent it shall upon occasion be abbreviated. The files should stand as in Corner Dances— about twelve feet apart.

HOW D'YE DO (CORNER DANCE).

This dance, as will be clearly seen from the Notation (*see* p. 75), serves as illustration of the national method of settling quarrels—by a bout of fisticuffs. All the dances are typical of the race; this one is of course singularly so. Where boys are found disposed to look favourably upon the Morris dance, "How d'ye do" may be recommended as the very best to encourage the tendency in them. There is a spice of wholesome rowdiness in the spirit of the dance that will not fail to make itself known and beloved of boys. Besides, the shaking of hands before the fight, the squaring-up for war, and the reconciliation, can only be given the right robustious ring and defiance by the fighting sex. Another most engaging feature of "How d'ye do," is that the notes fitting these words, as will be found, are sung in every instance by the dancers, before, during and after the encounter. There is plenty of room, there, for a different sounding of the phrase: for making it ring of challenge, and strife, and victory—also of honourable defeat, after lusty strokes have been dealt and taken: the next best thing to a win—sometimes even a better thing.

The following instructions for the dancing of "How d'ye do" must be noted in connection with the Notation (*see* p. 75).

The phrase "How d'ye do" is always sung, by all the couples, as marked and played in music "B." Opposite pairs advance as shown. They should meet together in the centre on the word "do," and shake hands, or square up for the fight, according to instructions.

Having joined hands, or squared, and paused in the centre, the first two pairs (Nos. 1 and 6, and 2 and 5) break away immediately after pause, and back briskly to their places, making room for the next pair. There is no changing of corners in this dance.

The last pair (Nos. 3 and 4) remain in position, holding hands or squaring up, during pause in music, and still remain in the attitude while bars 4 and 5 of "B" are played. During these bars all the other dancers stand still.

When the music strikes into "A" section, all take part according to instructions. Nos. 8 and 4 loose or lower hands immediately the "A" music starts, and take their place and part with the others.

SHEPHERD'S HEY.

STICK-TAPPING.

In this, the sticks are held in the fist, up and slanting outward, the top as high as the head. Partners cross sticks, leading file (Nos. 1, 3, and 5) holding to the right of even numbers. The tapping (or clashing, rather, for here the sticks are loudly clashed together) is done on first three beats of bars 1 and 2, and 5 and 6 of "B" music (*see* mark X). Partners strike each other's sticks, right, left, right, according to position, in the manner of sham fencing—the manner of brigands in pantomime.

While the tapping is being done all stand fast, not moving the feet at all. When the six taps are finished, in bars 1 and 2, 5 and 6, the sticks are held crossed and in position; and in bars 3 and 4, 7 and 8 all break into 4/3 step, and keep it up throughout those bars. The movement sounds absurdly simple: so it is, but if done with precision the effect is at once quaint and stirring.

HAND-CLAPPING.

This is done with the naked hands, handkerchiefs hanging loose from middle fingers; and dancers should clap hands as loudly as ever they can. Each dancer claps hands and knees in a number of different ways, according to explanation and diagram which follow. All stand fast while clapping, not moving the feet.

Each individual dancer--
Claps his hands together before him:
Shown thus in diagram which follows   b.
Or slaps right knee with right hand   r.k.
Or slaps left knee with left hand   l.k.
Or raises right knee and claps hands under it   un.r.
Or raises left knee and claps hands under it   un.l.
Or claps both hands together, behind him   b.beh.

DIAGRAM OF HAND-CLAPPING.

Hand-clapping in last four bars of "B" music is a repetition of clapping in first four bars, as shown in diagram. Therefore in the Notation of this dance (p. 77) the term "Hand-clapping" means clapping as shown above, and the same repeated.

ON HOLDING STICKS.

Unless specially instructed otherwise, the stick is held, whether at the end or middle, as follows. It must be grasped much as a penholder should be; that is, lying in the hollow at the base of the thumb, supported by the second finger, and with the forefinger and thumb meeting together above it, to hold it in place.

NOTATION.
MOVEMENTS. FORMA'
MUSIC.

BEAN SETTING (STICK DANCE).

In this dance, the step throughout is 4/2.

Once to yourself.	Partners tap across on last half-bar.	Column.
A. (1st time).	Ring (*see* p. 51). Partners tap across at half-bar in bars 4 and 8.	Col. to Ri
B.	Dibbing (*see* p.	Front.

MUSIC.	MOVEMENTS.	FORMATION.
	LAUDNUM BUNCHES (CORNER DANCE).	
Once to yourself.	Ju. last half-bar.	Column.
A.	Ju. last half-bar. Down-and-back, Ju. Up-and-back, j. (forming Fr.).	" Col. to F
B. (Corners).		
Bars 1, 2 and 3	Nos. 1 and 6 advance, at 6/3 step, and cross to each other's place.	Front.
Bar 4	Nos. 1 and 6 (having now changed corners), turn about, inward, at 6/3 step, till they face each other.	"
Bars 5 and 6	Nos. 1 and 6 advance, at 6/3 step, to centre, until they are face to face; they do not touch or pass.	"
Bars 7 and 8	Nos. 1 and 6 retire at 6/2 step, back to corners; and Ju. on half-bar of bar 8. They have now changed corners.	"
B. (Corners) (2nd time).	Nos. 2 and 5 change corners, precisely as Nos. 1 and 6 in B, 1st time.	"
B. (Centres) (3rd time).	Nos. 3 and 4 change places precisely as the others. Opposites *have now all* changed places.	"
A. (repeat).	Chain.	Column.
B. (Corners) (Repeat) 1st time.	Nos. 1 and 6 change corners as before.	Front.
B. (Corners) (Repeat) 2nd time.	Nos. 2 and 5 change corners as before.	"
B. (Centres) (Repeat) 3rd time.	Nos. 3 and 4 change places as before. Opposites have now all re-changed places.	"
A2.	Cross-over.	"
A. (2nd time).	Cross-over. Partners tap across at half-bar in bars 4 and 8, that is, at middle and end of the Cross-over.	"
B. (2nd time).	Dibbing.	"
A. (3rd time).	Back-to-back. Tap as in A. (2nd time).	"
B. (3rd time).	Dibbing. Two bars before the end, leader calls "All in," whereupon all, as they tap for the last time, j. outward, forming Column, and stand for a moment with sticks crossed. ALL IN.	"
C. (Capers) (1st time).		
Bar 1	Nos. 1 and 6 advance at 6/3 step towards the centre, facing each other's corners.	"
Bar 2 (9/8 time: 3 beats).	On beat 2, Nos. 1 and 6, their right shoulders now level, and almost touching, jump heavily on both feet, and advance, at 6/1 step, High, on beat 3.	"
Bar 3	Nos. 1 and 6 continue advance, 6/1, High.	"
Bar 4	Nos. 1 and 6 reach opposite corners and turn about to right and inward, same step.	"
Bar 5 (9/8 time: 3 beats).	Nos. 1 and 6 advance, 6/1, High, and come face to face on third beat.	"
Bars 6 and 7	Nos. 1 and 6 remain facing, and step at 6/3 step.	"
Bars 8 and 9	Nos. 1 and 6 retire to corners at 6/2 step. Ju. on half-bar of bar 9. Nos. 1 and 6 have now changed corners.	Front.
C. (Capers) (2nd time).	Nos. 2 and 5 change corners precisely as Nos. 1 and 6 in C, 1st time.	
C. (Capers)	Nos. 2 and 4 change places	"

	MOVEMENTS.	FORMATION.
(3rd time).	precisely as the others.	
A2. (repeat)	Back-to-back.	"
C. (Capers) (Repeat).	Movements as in first Capers. Opposites re-change places. But at the beginning of bar 6 of 3rd repeat, leader calls "All in," whereupon all turn inward, at 6/3 step, form Ring in the centre, raise the right feet; and on last beat, all throw up hands and Call.	Ring.

	MOVEMENTS.	FOR...
	COUNTRY GARDENS (HANDKERCHIEF DANCE).	
Once to yourself.	Ju. last half-bar.	Colu...
A1.	Down-and-back, Ju.	"
	Up-and-back, j. (forming Fr.).	Col. ...
B1.		
Bars 1 to 4.	Hand-striking as per Notation (see p. 58).	Front
Bars 5 to 8.	Half-chain.	Colu...
Bars 9 to 12.	Hand-striking.	Front
Bars 13 to 16.	Half-chain. This completes the Chain.	Colu...
C1.	Chain.	Colu...
B2.		
Bars 1 to 4.	Hand-striking.	Front
Bars 5 to 8.	Hand-striking, repeated.	"
A2.	Cross-over.	"
B3.		
Bars 1 to 4.	Hand-striking.	"
Bars 5 to 8.	Hand-striking, repeated	"
C2.	Back-to-back.	"
B4.		
Bars 1 to 4.	Hand-striking.	"
Bars 5 to 7.	Hand-striking, repeated. Beginning of bar 5, leader calls "All in."	"
Bar 8.	Beat 1, all j. (giving Col. formation). Half-bar, all throw up hands. ALL IN.	Colu...

	MOVEMENTS.	FORMA...
	CONSTANT BILLY (STICK DANCE).	
Once to yourself	Partners tap across, last half-bar.	Column.
A1.	Down-and-back, Ju.	"
	Up-and-back, j. (forming Front).	Col. to Fr...
	Partners tap at half-bar in bars 4 and 8.	
B1.		
Bars 1 to 4	Tapping (see diagram, p. 54).	"
Bars 5 to 8	Half-Chain. Tap on half-bar in bar 8.	Column.
Bars 9 to 12	Tapping, as in first 4 bars.	Front.
Bars 13 to 16	Complete Chain. Tap on last half-bar.	Column.
A2.	Chain. Tap at half-bar in bars 4 and 8.	"
B2.		
Bars 1 to 4	Tapping as before.	Front.
Bars 5 to 8	Tapping as before.	"
Bars 9 to 16	Cross-over. Tap at half-bar in bars 12 and 16.	"
A3.		
Bars 1 to 4	Tapping as before.	"
Bars 5 to 8	Tapping as before.	"
B3.		
Bars 1 to 8	Back-to-back. Tap as in Chain, &c.	"
Bars 9 to 12	Tapping as before.	Front.
Bars 13 to 16	Tapping as before; but in bar 14 leader calls "All in," and in bar 16 all j. (to Col.), and tap across on last half-bar, holding sticks as at the beginning. ALL IN.	" Column.

	MOVEMENTS.	FORMA...
	TRUNKLES (CORNER DANCE).	
Once to yourself	Ju, last half-bar.	Column.
A1.	Down-and-back, Ju., Up-and-back, j. (forming Fr).	Column
B1. (Corners).		
(1st time). Bars 1 to 8	Nos. 1 and 6 advance at 4/3 step, beginning with the left foot, so that they are face to face at the end of bar 3.	Front.
Bar 4	At beginning, Nos. 1 and 6 stamp their right feet.	

				1 and 6 Ju. Nos. 1 and 6 have now changed corners.	(repeat).	
	Nos. 1 and 6 raise and swing their right feet and on half-bar, strike them together, sidelong; then step briskly backward to their places, making room for Nos. 2 and 5.				**B2.** (repeat). (3 times).	As in B1 (repeat), pairs start with right feet so that, in bar 4, they stamp and strike the left feet. "
		C1. (Capers) (2nd time).	Nos. 2 and 5 change corners as Nos. 1 and 6 in C, 1st time.	"	**C2.** (repeat). (3 times). Capers. Slower.	As in C2. Pairs re-change. "
B1. (Corners). (2nd time).	Nos. 2 and 5 do precisely as Nos. 1 and 6 in B1, 1st time.	**C1.** (Capers) (3rd time).	Nos. 3 and 4 change places as Nos. 1 and 6 in C, first time.	"	**A3.** **B3.** (3 times).	Cross-over. " As in B1 and B2. " Pairs start with left feet, and stamp and strike right feet.
B1. (Centres). (3rd time).	Nos. 3 and 4 do precisely as Nos. 1 and 6 in B1, 1st time.	**A1.** (repeat). **B1.** (repeat). (3 times).	Chain. As before, with the difference only that pairs start with right foot so that, in bar 4, they stamp and strike together the left feet.	Column. Front.	**C3.** (Capers). (3 times). Bars 1, 2, 3, 4 in each repetition (very slow).	As in C1, pairs change places. In these the step " is 4/1, and High—really as high as possible.
C1. (Capers). (1st time). Bars 1 and 2	Nos. 1 and 6 advance at 4/3 step; pass in centre, right shoulders touching, and get to each other's places.	**C1.** (repeat). (3 times).	As before, All change places again, returning, therefore, to original stations.	Front.	Bars 5 and 6 in each repetition (presto).	In these the pairs retire, after meeting in centre, at 4/2 step, lifting the feet as high as possible, and as quickly. The greater the contrast between these two quick bars and the preceding slow ones, the better the effect. Front.
Bar 3	Nos. 1 and 6 turn about, inward and to the right, at 4/3 step.	**A2.** **B2.** (3 times).	Cross-over. As in B1. Pairs start with left feet, and stamp and strike right feet in bar 4.	" "		
Bar 4	Nos. 1 and 6 advance at 4/3 step until they come face to face, but do not touch or pass.	**C2.** (Capers). (3 times). Slower, except in last two bars, played in original time.	As in C1, except that pairs, in changing places, step rather higher to the slower music, also in the last two bars of normal time. The High Step is to be reserved for the Slow Capers in C3, and repeat.	"	**A3.** (repeat). **B3.** (repeat). (3 times).	Back-to-back. " As in B1 and B2 " (repeats), pairs start with right feet, and stamp and strike left feet in bar 4.
Bar 5	Nos. 1 and 6 retire, at 4/2 step, to opposite corners.					
Bar 6	Beginning, Nos. 1 and 6 reach opposite corners.					
	Half-bar, Nos.	**A2.**	Back-to-back.	"		

	MOVEMENTS.	FORMATION.
C3. (Capers) Very slow. (Repeat). (3 times).	As in C3. Pairs re-change to original places. At the beginning of bar 5, in final repetition of the music, leader calls "All in," when all draw together into Ring, throw up the right hands, raise the right feet, and Call. ALL IN.	" Fr. to R

MUSIC.

RIGS O' MARLOW (STICK DANCE).

	MOVEMENTS.	FORMATION.
Once to yourself	Tap sticks on last two beats of bar 4.	Column.
A. (1st time).	Step 4/2 throughout "A" music in all repetitions. Down-and-back twice. Partners tap sticks across on last two beats of bars 4 and 8; but on making last tap but one, j. (forming Fr.), so that final tap is given in Front formation.	" " Col. to Fr
B. (1st time).	Double-tapping. (For instructions, *see* diagram, 55).	Front.
A. (2nd time).	Chain. Tap sticks as in A, 1st time.	"
B. (2nd time).	Double-tapping, as in B, 1st time.	"
A. (3rd time).	Cross-over. Tap sticks as in A, 1st time.	"
B. (3rd time).	Double-tapping, as in B, 1st time.	"
A. (4th time).	Back-to back. Tap sticks as in A, 1st and 2nd time.	"
B. (4th time).	Double-tapping as in B, 1st and 2nd time. In bar 7, leader calls "All in," whereupon all j. , giving Col. formation, in which final tap is made. ALL IN.	" Column.

MOVEMENTS. FOR MUSIC.

BLUFF KING HAL

(HANDKERCHIEF DANCE.)

	MOVEMENTS.	FORMATION.
Once to yourself	None.	Front
A.		
Bars 1 to 4	Advance slowly, until files are face to face. On half-bar of bar 4, partners nod to one another (*see* instructions, 57).	"
Bars 5 to 8	Retire to original position.	Front
B.		
Bars 1 to 4	Mark time.	"
Bars 5 to 8	Advance and nod as before.	"
C.		
Bars 1 to 4	Retire.	"
Bars 5 to 8	Mark time. Files link arms in last bar, and remain linked until told to loose arms.	"
A.		
Bars 1 to 4	Advance as before, nod.	"
Bars 5 to 8	Retire.	"
B.		
Bars 1 to 4	Mark time.	"
Bars 5 to 8	Advance as before, nod.	"
C.		
Bars 1 to 4	Retire.	"
Bars 5 to 8	Loose arms. Files turn very slowly about until they are reversed.	"
A.		
Bars 1 to 4	Retire, until partners' backs are all but touching.	"
Bars 5 to 8	Advance to original position.	"
B.		
Bars 1 to 4	Mark time.	"
Bars 5 to 8	Retire as before.	"
C.		
Bars 1 to 4	Advance as before.	Front
Bars 5 to 8	Mark time. Link arms in last bar, and remain linked until told to loose arms.	"
A. B.	Go through same movements, linked, as in preceding A and B. Loose arms at end of B.	"
C.	Files extend into single line, facing music. To do this, Nos. 1 and 2 advance; Nos. 3 and 5 follow No. 1; Nos. 4 and 6 follow No. 2. When all are in line, with Nos. 1 and 2 at wings, Nos. 5 and 6 in centre, all face music. Distances	Line.

		between dancers to be kept the same as when in file.		Bars 1 to 4.	making double circuit.			DANCE).
A.				**B.**	Rings move to left,	"	Once to yourself.	Ju. last half-bar. Column.
Bars 1 to 4	Mark time.		"	Bars 5 to 8. and	as single Ring previously, nearly double circuit.		**A.**	
Bars 5 to 8	Advance.		"	**C.**			(1st time).	Down-and-back, Ju. Up-and-back., j. (forming Fr.). Column Front.
B.				Bars 1 to 4.				
Bars 1 to 4	Retire.		"	**C.**			**B.**	
Bars 5 to 8	Mark time.		"	Bars 5 to 8	Rings break up and re-form line of 6 as before.	Two Line.	(1st time) (Corners). Bar 1.	This is the Challenge. Nos. 1 and 6 advance and shake hands, as described (*see* p. 58). Front.
C.				**A. B. C.**	Line mark time, advance, retire, &c., as before, link arms in last bar of C.	Line.		
Bars 1 to 4	Advance.		"				Bar 2.	Nos. 2 and 5 the same. "
Bars 5 to 8	Retire. Link arms in last bar.		"	**A. B. C.**	Line as before, linked. Last 4 bars of C, break into files, in original position in Front, but reversed as before.	Line. Fron	Bar 3.	Nos. 3 and 4 the same. Front.
A. B.	Mark time, advance and retire linked, and mark time, as in preceding A and B. In last bar, loose arms and join hands.		"				Bar 4 and 5.	Nos. 3 and 4 pause (*see* p. 58). "
				A. B. C.	Files reversed, mark time, retire, advance, &c., as before. Link arms in last bar of C.	"	**A.**	
C.	Form into Ring: Nos. 1 and 2 joining hands in last bar.	Ring					(2nd time).	Chain. Column.
				A. B. C.	Files, reversed, mark time, retire, advance, &c., as before, arms linked. Loose arms, and turn slowly about in last 4 bars of C, forming Front.	"	**B.**	
A. (8 bars), and **B.** (Bars 1 to 4).	Move to right, dancers making the complete circle.		"				(2nd time) (Corners). Bar 1.	This is the Fight. Nos. 1 and 6 advance and square up, as shown in description (*see* p. 58). Front.
B. Bars 5 to 8, and **C.** Bars 1 to 4.	Move to left, dancers nearly travelling round circle again.		"	**A. B. C.**	Mark time, advance, nod, &c., as before. Link arms in last bar of C.	"	Bar 2.	Nos. 2 and 5 the same. "
							Bar 3.	Nos. 3 and 4 the same. "
C. Bars 5 to 8	Nos. 5 and 6 loose hands. No. 5 joins hands with No. 1, and No. 6 with No. 2, forming two rings, one to each file. Each ring will form round about the line of position of its numbers when in file.	Two		**A. B. C.**	Mark time, advance, &c., with linked arms, as before. At the call of "All in," the dance ends quietly on the last four bars, mark time, of C.	"	Bars 4 and 5.	Nos. 3 and 4 pause as before. "
							A. (3rd time.)	Cross-over. "
							B.	
				MUSIC.	**MOVEMENTS. FORMA**		(3rd time) (Corners).	This is the Reconciliation, and goes precisely as in B, 1st time. "
A. (8 bars) and **B.**	Rings move to right, as single Ring previously, but	Two		**HOW D'YE DO (CORNER**			**A.** (4th time).	Back-to-back. "

	MOVEMENTS.	FOR MUSIC.
B. (4th time) (Corners).	This is Good Fellowship, and goes precisely as in B, 1st and 3rd time.	"
A2.	Cross-over. As usual, up to bar 7, when leader calls "All in," whereupon all close inward into Ring in centre; throw up hands, raise right feet on last half-bar, and Call. ALL IN.	" Ring.
A3.	Go-and-come. j. on last half-bar (to Col.). To extend, repeat A1, B1, A2, B2 (2nd time).	Fr. to Col.
A3. (repeat). (*Presto*).	Dance at 4/3 quick-step, mark time (that is, in position); left hand hanging loose, until last half-bar, when it is thrown up. Right hand holds stick across the body, the stick slanting upward towards the right shoulder. Two bars from end leader calls "All in." All Ju. on last half-bar, and throw up both hands. ALL IN.	Colun

SHEPHERD'S HEY
(STICK OR HANDKERCHIEF DANCE).

	MOVEMENTS.	FOR MUSIC.
Once to yourself.	Ju. last half-bar.	Colun
A1.	Down-and-back, Ju. Up-and-back, j. (forming Fr.)	" Col.
B1.	Tapping (or Hand-clapping). (*See* p. 59.)	Front.
A2.	Chain.	Colun
B2.	Tapping (or Hand-clapping).	Front.
A1. (2nd time).	Go-and-come.	"
B1. (2nd time).	Tapping (or Hand-clapping).	"
A2. (2nd time).	Back-to-back.	"
B2. (2nd time).	Tapping (or Hand-clapping).	"

BLUE-EYED STRANGER
(HANDKERCHIEF DANCE).

	MOVEMENTS.	FOR MUSIC.
Once to yourself.	Ju. last half-bar.	Colu
A1.	Down-and-back, Ju. Up-and-back, j. (forming Fr.)	" Col.
B1. Bars 1 to 8.	All dance at 4/3 step, mark time; swinging hands back and forth together in time. Bars 7 and 8 to be danced in 4/2 step.	Front
B1. Bars 9 to 16.	Chain.	Colu
A2.	As previously in B1, bars 1 to 8.	Front
B2. Bars 1 to 8.	Cross-over.	"
B2. Bars 9 to 16.	As previously in B1, bars 1 to 8.	"
A1. (2nd time).	Back-to-back.	"
B1. Bars 1 to 8. (2nd time).	As previously in B1, bars 1 to 8, until bar 7, when leader call "All in." All then draw into Ring in centre, throw up hands on half-bar of bar 8, and Call. (To extend this dance to full length of music, (*see* p. 50) ALL IN.	" Fr. to Ring

MORRIS OFF.

This, as the name denotes, is the tune to which the dancers step as they leave the scene—be it stage, or high road, or village green—of their performance. Its execution is very simple, and there is no limit to the number of times the eight-bar measure may be played—or rather, the limit is set according to the fancy of the leader, for he may, if he pleases, and if the audience manifests no impatience, lead his side back and forth in a serpentine track, round and round for ever so long, till finally they wind from the scene.

The step is the 4/3 step throughout, but with a difference. It is more of a plod, with less of stamping and much less lifting of the feet. Morris Off, danced in the traditional manner, gives one the impression of a company agreeably tired, but pleased and comfortable, having rollicked to their hearts' content, and to the contentment of the lookers-on; and being now upon the way to supper, and to bed. Of course, if they be still exuberant, they may show it, and stamp their lustiest; still a demurer step will usually suggest itself as the more appropriate. This quieter manner is best described as almost a slow, very gentle trot, the steps little longer than the foot—left, right, left; and then, on the fourth beat, not a hop, but a tap with the heel.

As for the movements. After "Once to yourself," the side marks time for 6 bars, and makes a complete right turn, slowly, in bars 7 and 8; then the leader, with Nos. 3 and 5 behind him, starts forward as described, Nos. 2, 4 and 6 meanwhile marking time. As No. 5 draws level with No. 2, he falls in behind, and Nos. 4 and 6 in order after him.

The side is now going slowly forward, in the manner of "Follow my leader." In every repetition of bars 7 and 8, all make a complete right turn, as already described, so that at the repeat of the first bar all are again facing in the course the leader shall have set.

The course will be set according to circumstances, and the position of exit, if in a room; or, if in the open, the leader will wind—or in the old manner of saying, he will "hey"— to some chosen point for quitting the scene.

To hey was to wind in and out and round about—though the term has many meanings. That is the leader's business: to lead the side across and back again, all turning together in the last two bars, and back and across again, or round about occasionally, as long as he may please.

Suppose more than one side has been dancing; then the leading side will start as already described, the other, or others, falling in as may have been previously arranged.

Morris Off, smoothly and quietly danced, with its strange monotony, has a fascination all its own. It is farewell, with no sorrow in it; good-bye, but with no dread of loneliness tomorrow; somehow, one cannot tell how, all the wholesomeness of the Morris, and of the folk that sent it down to us, and are with us yet, is in this dance. When the dance is over, and the bells quiet, there is neither surfeit nor exhaustion. Morris Off is like to make one think of sound sleep and clear awakenings.